Historic Pipe Organs of the Keeweenaw
Houghton County, Michigan

The Keweenaw is unique in that it has fourteen historic pipe organs still in service. This booklet gives a history of those organs in Houghton County and a brief history of the churches that house these treasures. Thanks to the following organizations, community members, and churches that have worked to preserve and maintain these beautiful instruments:

The Calumet Art Center - Calumet, MI
First United Methodist Church - Hancock, MI
Gloria Dei Lutheran Church - Hancock, MI
Grace United Methodist Church - Houghton, MI
Houghton County Historical Society - Lake Linden, MI
Keweenaw Heritage Center at St. Anne's - Calumet, MI
Lake Linden United Methodist Church - Lake Linden, MI
St. Albert the Great Catholic Church - Houghton, MI
St. John's Lutheran Church - Hubbell, MI
St. Joseph's Catholic Church - Lake Linden, MI
St. Paul the Apostle Catholic Church - Calumet, MI
St. Paul's Evangelical Lutheran Church - Laurium, MI
Trinity Episcopal Church - Houghton, MI
David & Carol Waisanen - Hancock, MI

Printing of this booklet is made possible by a grant from the Keweenaw National Historical Park Advisory Commission and generous donations from the organizations above, Jan Dalquist, Ed & Liz Sheridan, and Ron & Barb Eckoff.

Copyright 2012
Isle Royale & Keweenaw Parks Association
Houghton, Michigan
www.irkpa.org

A Tribute

David Short and Jan Dalquist were the inspiration for this booklet. Our community has been blessed by their years of devotion to organ music and playing in local churches. Both have done in-depth research into the historic organs of the Keweenaw, resulting in Jan's published article in *The Diapason* in February 2007.

David Short has been playing for church services and public events since the sixth grade. He is largely self-taught and has developed his own system to read the music written by others. He writes:

"As a kid I had the ability to hear the music, put it through my limited system and play it back as if I had learned it properly. It was the 'D. L. Short Treatment of a Melody.' The only ones I couldn't fool were the trained musicians…and that never set well with me. By nature I am an entertainer, by conviction I am indebted to the composers who gave us our treasury of music. We want to respect Buxtehude, Bach, Franck and all the others for pointing us toward God and musical excellence. We need to bask in their intelligence and artistry."

Jan Dalquist has been playing for worship services since she was twelve years of age. Her first organ lessons were during high school at the Kilgen organ in the Menominee Presbyterian church. She minored in music with emphasis on organ at Macalester College in St. Paul; Harriet Allen of the McPhail School of Music was her teacher.

After graduation, Dalquist married and earned her Masters in Christian Education from McCormick Seminary. Three children—and a Masters in Library Science from the University of Michigan—followed. She spent thirty years as an academic librarian, occasionally substituting for various organists during that time.

In 1989, she became the regular organist at the Portage Lake United Church. Dalquist has continued her study of the organ through organ workshops held at St. Olaf College, the University of Michigan, and at local venues. The church library includes 100 essays on hymns and worship, Dalquist's primary interest.

Dalquist and Short are charter members of the Organists of the Keweenaw (also known simply as the Organists). The group organized after the Pine Mountain Music Festival (PMMF) held an organ workshop in 1995. It was through Short's interest in the Keweenaw's historic pipe organs that the Organists were introduced to these instruments. Since that time, group members have played recitals on most of the organs, and several have helped restore the instruments at the Houghton County Museum in Lake Linden and the Keweenaw Heritage Center in Calumet. The PMMF continues to sponsor master classes and lessons year after year, but the Organists have also independently hosted several nationally recognized organ teachers and performers: local organists have had the benefit of working with some of the best this country has to offer.

3

Historic Pipe Organs of the Keweenaw
Houghton County, Michigan
By Anita Campbell & Jan Dalquist

History

The Keweenaw Peninsula, the northernmost part of Michigan's Upper Peninsula, projects into Lake Superior, and in 1844 was the site of the first copper rush in the United States.

As large numbers of immigrants flocked to the Keweenaw to work in the copper mines, they brought their music with them. They shared working songs, drinking songs, folk songs, and parlor songs. Much of what defined ethnic identity and culture through the decades of the 19th and early 20th century were the hymns learned in church, where the organ was, and remains, the song leader.

During the early years of copper mining, reed pump organs were common in both church and home. Most likely, congregations that could not afford pipe organs bought reed organs instead. Some of these instruments, now over 100 years old, still survive in the Keweenaw. At least two are currently used during the summer months in local chapels. Others, also in working order, can be seen in local museums.

The magnificent pipe organs highlighted in this booklet hold a valuable history. They reflect the most prosperous years in the Keweenaw when people of wealth sought the best music for their churches and arranged for the purchase of these instruments.

The Keweenaw boasts pipe organs dating from 1870 to 1968. All are in working order and in regular use. Several are in their original state, having been installed with electric blowers and with either electro-pneumatic or electro-magnetic action. Some have been so enlarged over time, with additional pipes and digital circuitry that they no longer resemble the original instrument. Several are tracker organs. All of them have electric blowers, but four can still be hand pumped. One of the trackers has a detached and reversed keydesk. Only one organ has three manuals. One has an echo organ placed at the opposite end of the sanctuary from the main organ chamber. Another is a beautiful one-manual, no-pedalboard organ with fully exposed pipes.

Over the years, conscientious congregations and community groups have attended to the maintenance of these historic pipe organs. As a group, they are an irreplaceable treasure, a legacy from the people who sought to bring the best of instruments to their churches for their peoples' song. These are instruments worthy of preservation, care, and constant use. Let them be heard!

Lake Linden United Methodist Church

St. Albert the Great Catholic Church
411 MacInnes Drive, Houghton, MI 49931
Phone: (906) 482-5530

Church History

During the late 1950s, as the Catholic Newman and Aquinas Clubs at Houghton's Michigan College of Mining and Technology were outgrowing their facility at 1301 Ruby Avenue (where Phi Kappa Theta fraternity is located), plans were conceived to build a new chapel and student center on campus. It was decided that the new center should have a patron saint: St. Albert the Great (1206-1280), Doctor of the Church, who as patron of the natural scientists made his love of truth about nature into an instrument of his love of Christ. On October 6, 1963, the cornerstone was laid for our parish, which is entrusted to the patronage of St. Albert the Great.

Organ History

Felgemaker, Erie, Pennsylvania, 1882/c.1905/2011, 2M, 12 ranks, tracker. Hand pump preserved.

This organ was constructed around 1882 by the A. B. Felgemaker Co. in Erie, Pennsylvania, for a church in Manitowoc, Wisconsin. Sometime after 1905, the organ was relocated to St. Cecilia's Catholic Church in Hubbell, Michigan, which had been built in 1893. St. Cecilia's parish provided for German, French, and Irish immigrants, and was an offshoot of St. Joseph's Church in Lake Linden. The church featured a stained glass window of St. Cecilia, the patron saint of church music, playing an organ. St. Cecilia's Catholic Church was closed in 2007 and the organ moved to St. Albert the Great Catholic Church in Houghton in 2011. Restoration work was done by Lauck Organ Building Co. of Otsego, Michigan, and several congregational volunteers.

This included restoration of the feeder bellows and pipes that had been damaged, regulating keyboards, and rebuilding the pedals. The casework was completely refinished by Fr. Al's mother, Jan Mott.

At the dedication of the organ, Bishop Sample emphasized how this pipe organ on the campus of Michigan Technological University would educate generations of students about the sacred music of the church. (Source: David Short and Fr. Al Mott)

GREAT
8'   Open Diapason
8'   Flute
8'   Dulciana
4'   Octave
2'   Super Octave
16' Bourdon
Bellows Signal

SWELL
8'   Stopped Diapason
8'   Viola
8'   Aolina
4'   Flute Harmonique
8'   Oboe

PEDAL
16' Bourdon
Couplers
Swell to Great
Swell to Pedal
Great to Pedal
Tremolo St.

7

Grace United Methodist Church
201 Isle Royale Street, Houghton, MI 49931
Phone: (906) 482-2780

Church History

Grace Church, Houghton's first organized religious body, grew out of a "Methodist Class" formed in 1854. The "class" was an extension of Methodist missionary activity to the Ojibwa of Keweenaw Bay, which had expanded to include Cornish Methodist immigrants to the region's newly opened copper mines.

The congregation erected a wooden building on the site of the present church in 1859, replacing it with a larger Jacobsville sandstone structure in 1893, at the height of the region's mining prosperity. Fire gutted the interior in 1916, with repairs completed only in 1925. In 1991 the congregation expanded the 1893 structure to the south, roughly doubling its area.

Organ History

Maxcy-Barton, 1931; rebuilt by Verlinden Company, 1971.

The church had an organ by the 1880s at the latest, and probably acquired a new one when the church expanded in 1893. This organ, however, was destroyed in the 1916 fire.

In 1931 the congregation purchased a Maxcy-Barton organ. The somewhat smaller Maxcy-Barton of the First Presbyterian Church was likely installed in the same era since the organs are otherwise similar. In 1971 Verlinden Company rebuilt the instrument, and in the 1990s the console was removed from the dais at the front of the church to the main floor level on the left side of the chancel. (Source: Terry Reynolds)

GREAT
8'	Open Diapason
8'	Melodia
8'	Salicional
8'	Dulciana
4'	Octave
4'	Wald Flute
4'	Dulcet
22/3'	Twelfth
2'	Fifteenth
16'	Great to Great
4'	Great to Great
8'	Swell to Great
4'	Swell to Great
	Chimes

PEDAL
16'	Sub Bass
16'	Bourdon
8'	Octave
8'	Bass Flute
8'	Bourdon
8'	Cello
4'	Choral Bass
4'	Flute
8'	Great to Pedal
8'	Swell to Pedal
4'	Great to Pedal

SWELL
16'	Bourdon
8'	Stopped Flute
8'	Salicional
8'	Dulciana
8'	Vox Celeste
4'	Principal
4'	Flute d'Amour
4'	Salicet
22/3'	Nazard
2'	Flautino
13/5'	Tierce
8'	Orchestral Oboe
16'	Swell to Swell
4'	Swell to Swell
	Unison Off
	Tremulant

3 pistons and cancel on Swell
3 pistons and cancel on Great
One toe stud, coupler
1 expression pedal
1 crescendo pedal

9

Trinity Episcopal Church
205 East Montezuma Avenue, Houghton, MI 49931
Phone: (906) 482-2010

Church History

The Episcopal congregation in Houghton-Hancock formed in 1860. The parish was officially founded in 1861 when the congregation entered into an agreement with members of the Congregational denomination to jointly construct a building in Hancock. However, disagreement followed regarding the denomination to which the building would be dedicated.

The Episcopalians, who comprised the majority of the joint church board, prevailed, and the wooden building was floated across Portage Lake to Houghton to the site of the present church. Construction on the present church began in 1907. The first service was held on Easter 1910, and the building was consecrated later that year.

Organ History

The organ was built by the Austin Organ Company of Hartford, Connecticut, using the Universal Air Chest System. It was installed in 1912, and comprises three manuals and pedal and twenty-five stops, the equivalent of an ordinary thirty stop organ.

The summary of specifications are: 3 manuals, 25 speaking stops, 20 couplers, 18 adjustable combinations, pistons, 3 adjustable pedals, 5 pedal movement, 4 piston movements. The key action is electric and stop action electro-pneumatic. In 1957-58 a new console was installed with the addition of three new stops. In 1924 an echo organ was installed in the rear of the church.

GREAT
8'	Open Diapason	Rank 1
8'	Clarabella	Rank 2
8'	Dulciana	Choir
4'	Octave	Rank 3
4'	Stopped Flute	Choir
2'	Fifteenth	(ext. of Rank 1)
III	Mixture	Ranks 4,5,6

Great 16
Great 4
Great Unison Off
Swell to Great 16, 8, 4
Choir to Great 16, 8, 4
Echo on Great
Echo on Great Off
Chimes (Echo) 25 bars

SWELL
16'	Bourdon	Rank 12
8'	Rohrflute	Rank 13
8'	Viole d'Orchestre	Rank 14
4'	Geigen Principal	Rank 15
4'	Flute Harmonique	Rank 16
2 2/3'	Nazard	Rank 17
2'	Flautino	Rank 18
8'	Cornopean	Rank 19
8'	Oboe	Rank 20

Tremolo
Swell 16, 4
Swell Unison Off

CHOIR
8'	Violin Cello	Rank 7
8'	Spitzflute	Rank 8
8'	Dulciana	Rank 9
4'	Flute	Rank 10
8'	Clarinet	Rank 11

Tremolo
Choir 16, 8, 4
Choir Unison Off
Swell to Choir

ECHO
8'	Chimney Flute	Rank 21
8'	Viole Aetheria	Rank 22
8'	Vox Angelica	Rank 23
4'	Fern Flute	Rank 24
8'	Cor Anglais	Rank 25
8'	Vox Humana	Rank 26

Tremolo
Chimes   25 bars
16'   Pedal Bourdon (ext. of Rank 21)

PEDAL
32'	Resultant Bass	Wired
16'	Open Diapason (ext. of Rank 1)	
16'	Bourdon	Rank 27
16'	Contra Dulciana (ext. of Rank 9)	
16'	Gedeckt	Swell
8'	Flute	(ext. of Rank 27)
16'	Echo Bourdon (ext. of Rank 21)	

Great to Pedal 8, 4
Swell to Pedal 8, 4
Choir to Pedal 8, 4

Programmable thumb pistons under each manual
Toe pistons: 10 General; 5 Pedal with some reversibles
Crescendo pedal
Swell expression
Choir expression
Choir & Great are on same wind chest

First Presbyterian Church
Houghton, Michigan (no longer standing)

Church History

Founded on May 3, 1903, the Presbyterian Church was located on the southeast corner of College Avenue and Franklin Street. Constructed of Jacobsville sandstone, it featured flying buttresses, modified gothic arches and cathedral glass windows. Many of Houghton's influential families were members of the church.

Relocation of Montezuma Ave. meant the church would be demolished. Concurrently, the Hancock Congregational Church was structurally unsound. Both buildings were razed. On June 8, 1969, the two congregations merged to form Portage Lake United Church.

Organ History

Maxcy-Barton, Oshkosh, WI, 2M, 8 ranks, 1931-33?, electro-pneumatic; installed by owner, 1975.

This organ was originally installed in the First Presbyterian Church, Houghton, between 1931 and 1933. It is believed that at the same time, a larger Maxcy-Barton was placed in the Grace Methodist Church. Maxcy organs were custom built to fit the acoustics of the space. The organ chamber in the Presbyterian Church was at the front of the sanctuary and enclosed in a wooden grillwork similar to the one in Grace. The detached console was located below the rostrum and in front of the choir loft, which was an elevated tiered area at one side of the chancel. Organists on the Maxey-Barton organ were Kathryn Bree, James Abrams, and Isabelle Hagen. The church was known for its choral programs.

David & Carol Waisanen of Hancock, Michigan, purchased the organ in 1976 and installed in their home in 1977-78.

The organ chamber is enclosed in the original wood grillwork from the church and the console sits on what used to be the back porch of their home. (Sources: *The Daily Mining Gazette*; Carol Waisanen)

GREAT
8'	Open Diapason	61 pipes
8'	Melodia	73 pipes
8'	Dulciana	61 pipes
4'	Flute	61 notes
	Unison Off	

SWELL
8'	Stopped Diapason	73 pipes
8'	Salicional	73 pipes
8'	Vox Humana	61 pipes
4'	Flute d'Amour	61 notes
	Tremulant	
	Unison Off	

PEDAL
16'	Bourdon	12 pipes
	(20 notes from Sw St. Diap.)	
8'	Flute (from Sw St. Diap.)	

Balanced expression pedal
Balanced adjustable
   crescendo pedal

Couplers
16'	Great to Great
4'	Great to Great
16'	Swell to Great
8'	Swell to Great
4'	Swell to Great
8'	Great to Pedal
8'	Swell to Pedal

Combination pistons:

3 Swell, controlling Swell and Pedal organs and couplers, cancel

3 Great, controlling Great and Pedal organs and couplers, cancel

First United Methodist Church
401 Quincy Street, Hancock, MI 49930
Phone: (906) 482-4190

Church History

The First United Methodist Church of Hancock, Michigan, is the city's oldest religious institution, having been founded in the winter of 1860-1861. The first church was built on the corner of Hancock and Ravine Streets.

A serious fire broke out on Sunday, April 11, 1869, which was reported to be the most awful spectacle the Copper Country citizens had ever witnessed. Only a small fringe of buildings survived on the north and west, among which the St. Patrick's and Methodist Churches loomed up like monuments marking the graves of their neighbors.

The church continued to serve the congregation until 1903 when a more central location and larger building were deemed advisable. The present structure of Jacobsville sandstone and brick was built and dedicated in 1903. (Source: 140th anniversary booklet, Carol Waisanen, music director)

Organ History

Kimball, 1905, tracker, 2M, 11 ranks; rebuilt to electro-pneumatic action 1950; new wind lines 1998; refurbished 2005 by Fabry Organ Building Company of Antioch, Illinois.

In 1905 the Kimball tracker organ was installed, a gift from Mr. & Mrs. W. H. Roberts. The console was built into the paneling of the chamber, with the choir loft on either side and in front and the organist's back to the choir and congregation.

In 1950 the organ was converted to electro-pneumatic and the console moved from its tracker position to a well at the opposite side of the choir loft. In 1998 the sanctuary was renovated and the choir loft was leveled to make a flat dais across the chancel area. The organ console was placed on a moveable platform, and new wind lines installed by Fabry, Inc. In 2005 Fabry also replaced slide tuners in the pipes, installed a new blower, and repainted the pipes located above the paneling fronting the lower part of the chamber. (Sources: Clarence Monette, Carol Waisanen)

GREAT
8'   Open Diapason
8'   Melodia 8'Dulciana
4'   Principal
4'   Flute
2 2/3'   Twelfth
2'   15th
4'   Great to Great
16'   Swell to Great
8'   Swell to Great
4'   Swell to Great

SWELL
8'   Violin Diapason
8'   Stopped Diapason
8'   Gamba
4'   Flute d'Amour
2 2/3'   Nazard
2'   Flautino
Tremolo
16'   Swell to Swell
4'   Swell to Swell

PEDAL
16'   Bourdon
16'   Gedeckt
8'   Principal
8'   Bass Flute
4'   Flute
8'   Great to Pedal
4'   Great to Pedal
8'   Swell to Pedal

Placement: front left dais; console is on a moveable platform

Console: not AGO, but radiating pedalboard.

15

Gloria Dei Lutheran Church (ELCA)
1000 Quincy Street, Hancock, MI 49930
Phone: (906) 482-2381

Church History

The Gloria Dei congregation traces its roots to 1867, when the Scandinavian Evangelical Lutheran Congregation was formed. It was reorganized in 1880 as the Finnish Evangelical Lutheran Congregation.

The first wood frame building was partly destroyed by fire in 1896 and again in 1909. A brick building was constructed in 1910. In 1955 the name of the church was changed to St. Matthew's Evangelical Lutheran Church.

In 1962 some of the national Lutheran church bodies merged into the Lutheran Church of America. Salem Lutheran (Swedish), which still stands today on the corner of Michigan Street and Highway 41, then merged with St. Matthew's (Finnish) in 1966 and adopted the name Gloria Dei. The present building was constructed in 1969.

Organ History

Kilgen, 1915c, 2M; moved to new building, 1969; console rebuilt and preparation made for additions, Fabry 2002.

Shortly after the building was constructed in 1910, a member of the congregation, Andrew Johnson, gave the first pipe organ to the church. The Kilgen organ from St. Matthew's was moved and installed in the new Gloria Dei Church in 1969.

In 2002 the organ was rebuilt by Fabry Inc, of Fox Lake, Illinois. (Sources: Clarence Monette; church records and members)

Placement: rear balcony; left side of console faces front of sanctuary.

GREAT		**SWELL**		**PEDAL**	
8'	Diapason	8'	Violin Diapason	32'	Resultant
8'	Gedeckt	8'	Gedeckt	16'	Bourdon
8'	Dulciana	8'	Salicional	16'	Lieblich Gedeckt
4'	Principal	8'	Voix Celeste	8'	Diapason
4'	Flute d'Amour	4'	Principal	8'	Bass Flute
4'	Dulcet	4'	Flute d'Amour	8'	Gedeckt
12th	Dolce	22/3'	Nazard	4'	Choral Bass
15th	Dolce	2'	Flautino	8'	Great to Pedal
13/5'	Dolce Tierce	8'	Trompette	8'	Swell to Pedal
16'	Great to Great	8'	Oboe	4'	Great to Pedal
4'	Great to Great		Tremolo	4'	Swell to Pedal
16'	Swell to Great	16'	Swell to Swell		
8'	Swell to Great	4'	Swell to Swell		
4'	Swell to Great		Unison Off		

GREAT (cont.):
Chimes
Unison Off
MIDI to Great

Memory Select
Transposer
Swell presets: 5, Swell to Pedal
Great presets: 5, Great to Pedal
Generals: 10, Tutti

Toe studs:
General cancel
10 Generals
Swell to Pedal
Great to Pedal
Resultant
Tutti

17

Houghton County Historical Society Heritage Center

(former First Congregational Church)
53102 Highway M-26, Lake Linden, MI 49945
Phone: (906) 296-4121

Church History

The Lake Linden First Congregational Church was built in 1896 at the cost of $8,325. A museum piece in itself, the building was designed by Holabird & Roche of Chicago in the Victorian Stick style on a non-coursed mine-rock foundation. It was dedicated on February 27, 1887, with the dedicatory service being played by Professor Roney, organist of the Michigan Grand Commander of the Knights Templar.

A fire destroyed almost all of Lake Linden in 1887, but the frame Congregational Church survived. It housed eight families for several months until new homes were found. The congregation ceased as a church in 1979, and ownership was taken over by the Houghton County Historical Museum. Grants have helped to renovate plumbing, roofing, electrical wiring, heating, and repainting of the outside of the building.

Organ History

Garret House, Buffalo, NY, 1873-74, 2M/23 stops, hand pump preserved, tracker installed 1887.

Dana Hull, Ann Arbor representative of the Organ Historical Society, and Helmut Schick of the University of Michigan cleaned and restored the organ

during 2001 and 2002. A new blower replaced the original. (Sources: Richard Taylor, *The Daily Mining Gazette*).

"Beautifully made, much detail and care; shows growth and refinement in an organ shipped to the hinterlands; finials, medallions in the casework, nice lines in the presentation; some expensive wood here and there, very well cut and finished, excellent pipework." (Source: email from David Short quoting Dana Hull and Helmut Schick 10-4-01)

GREAT
8'   Open Diapason
8'   Viol d'Aour (TC)
8'   Stopped Diapason Bass
8'   Melodia
4'   Flute
4'   Principal
2'   Fifteenth
     Tremolo

COUPLERS
Swell to Great
Great to Pedal
Swell to Pedal

hand pump

SWELL
8'   Open Diapason
8'   Clarabella (TC)
8'   Stopped Diapason Bass
8'   Stopped Diapason Treble
4'   Violina
8'   Hautboy (TC)

PEDAL
16' Bourdon

St. Joseph's Roman Catholic Church
701 Calumet Street, Lake Linden MI 49945
Phone: (906) 296-6851

Church History

The St. Joseph congregation was founded in 1871, and the first church was built the same year. The congregation was mostly French Canadian, with many people emigrating from Trois-Rivieres in Quebec.

The present structure was built in the early 1900s with sandstone from the local Jacobsville quarries. Services were held in the ground level "hall" until the superstructure was complete.

In 2002 the worship space was restored to a concept very much as it had been intended in the 1930s. Old photos were used in the planning of this restoration.

Organ History

Casavant Freres Opus 41, 1916 tubular pneumatic, 2M/23 stops, 25 ranks, electro-pneumatic.

The Casavant organ was installed in the rear gallery in 1916. Some of the pipes were probably from Canada, but many were certainly from South Haven, Michigan, as was the console and case. Pipe Organ Craftsmen of Minneapolis did maintenance work in 1957.

By 1980 the pneumatics were so compromised that it was decided an electric action should be installed. Verlinden Co. did this work in 1982. In 1996 Hebert and Son from Detroit cleaned the organ and installed a new console specially built for the instrument.

In 2000 the great, swell, and pedals divisions were all completed with the addition of 12 new ranks of pipes. These pipes were made and installed by Lauck Organ Company of Otsego, Michigan. The 1996 console had been prepared for these additions. (Source: David Short)

GRAND-ORGUE
8'	Montre	65 pipes
8'	Melodia	65 pipes
8'	Dulciana	65 pipes
4'	Prestant	61 pipes
2 2/3'	Quint*	61 pipes
2'	Doublette*	61 pipes
III	Fourniture*	183 pipes
8'	Trompette*	61 pipes
4'	Grand-Orge to Grand-Orgue	

RÉCIT (enclosed)
8'	Principal	65 pipes
8'	Bourdon	65 pipes
8'	Viola di Gamba	65 pipes
8'	Voix Céleste	53 pipes
4'	Flute Harmonique	65 pipes
2'	Octavin*	61 pipes
II	Sesquialtera TC*	98 pipes
8'	Hautbois	65 pipes
4'	Chalumeau*	61 pipes
	Tremulant	
4'	Récit to Récit	

PEDALE
16'	Bourdon	30 pipes
16'	Gedeckt	30 pipes
8'	Flute Bouchee	12 pipes
4'	Prestant	32 pipes
16'	Bombarde*est G-O	12 pipes
4'	Chalumeau	Recit

TIRASSES
8'	Grand-Orgue/Pedale
4'	Grand-Orgue/Pedale
8'	Recit/Pedale
4'	Recit/Pedale
16'	Recit/Grand Orgue
8'	Recit/Grand Orgue
4'	Recit/Grand Orgue

* Added stops 2001
23 stops, 25 ranks, 2340 pipes

Combination pistons:
6 thumb pistons, Swell
8 thumb pistons, Great
6 thumb pistons, Pedal
8 general pistons (thumb/toe)
8 memory levels - Peterson

Lake Linden United Methodist Church
53237 N Avenue, Lake Linden, MI 49945
Phone: (906) 296-0148

Church History

Two missionaries from the Detroit circuit began leading services in Lake Linden in 1868. Meetings were held in a former Ojibwa trading post sited at the head of Torch Lake. In 1870, the congregation began to use the one-room schoolhouse that stood where the current high school stands. Services alternated Sunday worship with the Catholic church until the first St. Joseph's Catholic Church was built in 1871. The first Methodist church was built in 1874, but by 1885 the congregation had outgrown it. They built the current Methodist church in 1886, dedicating it on November 7 of that year. Many current members of the church are fourth- and fifth-generation descendants of the original congregation. (Source: Church history compiled by Mr. August Hagen, November 5, 1911. Copyrighted 1931)

Organ History

Lancashire-Marshall, Moline, IL, 1893, $2,100, 2M/19 ranks, tracker pneumatic assist pedal: Hugh Stahl, 1950

When the organ was installed in 1893, it was considered something of a wonder. At one point, an organist traveled to Lake Linden from Houghton and stayed the day so as to play both morning and evening services.

The organ was originally winded by hand, and the blower was installed after World War I, much earlier than work done by Stahl. It is thought he may have worked on the pneumatics in the two pedal ranks, possibly doing needed repairs, and affixed the company tab to the keydesk at that time. Roscoe Wheeler of Iron Mountain, Michigan, did maintenance on the organ for many years prior to James Lauck taking over in 2001. (Source: email from David Short 2-14-06)

Placement: center front of chancel, keydesk back of pulpit facing the case.

GREAT (58 notes)
8'	Open Diapason
8'	Dulciana
8'	Melodia
4'	Octave
4'	Flute Harmonique
22/3'	Twelfth
2'	Fifteenth
16'	Trompette
	Tremolo
	Pedal Check
	Bellows Signal

PEDAL
(27 notes) (Pneumatic)
16'	Bourdon
8'	Flute

COUPLERS
Swell to Great
Swell to Pedal
Great to Pedal

SWELL (enclosed)
16'	Lieblich Gedact
16'	Bourdon Bass
8'	Open Diapason
8'	Stopped Diapason
8'	Aeoline
8'	Salicional
4'	Flauto Traverso
4'	Fugara
2'	Flautino
8'	Oboe

5-pedal presets, loud to soft
Original cost: $2,100
Additional work done by Hugh Stahl

St. John's Lutheran Church
26847 13th Street, Hubbell, MI 49945
Phone: (906) 296-1022

Church History

The church was formed on May 15, 1893 by twelve men who gave the congregation the name "Saint Johannes Congregation." The white frame building was dedicated on August 13, 1893. The first organ was purchased in 1894. Also in that same year, the congregation was incorporated and became a member of the Lutheran Church–Missouri Synod. In 1899 the interior of the church was covered with corrugated tin. In 1900 electric lights were installed. The basement was built in 1903.

After 1927, St. John's was without a resident pastor. Pastors from Hancock and Laurium served until 1942, when it joined St. Paul's in Laurium to form a dual parish.

Organ History

Verlinden Co., 1M, 5 ranks, 1968, Roscoe Wheeler, Iron Mountain, MI.

The organ was installed by Verlinden Co. in 1968. The open pipes of this unique instrument are mounted in the rear gallery of the sanctuary. The rope for the steeple bell descends amidst the pipes. The console is placed at one end of the gallery. The first part of the dedication service in November 1968 was played on the existing electronic instrument. During the service, Pastor Frank J. Schulz demonstrated the newly installed pipe organ, and the remainder of the service was played on that instrument. A 2' flute rank was added in 1977 as a memorial to the longtime organist.

The organ was rebuilt during 2006 by B.K. Kellogg & Assoc. Relay switches, console stop controls, key contacting systems and wiring were replaced. The leather on the wind regulator, the tremulant, and the wooden pipe stoppers were renewed, interior actions were reconditioned as needed, and one rank of pipes was added at a total cost of $16,000. (Source: email from organist June Peterson, 2-4-06)

Stoplist (257 pipes)

8'   Open Diapason
8'   Flute
8'   String
4'   Flute
2'   Flute
4'   Coupler
16'   Coupler
Tremulant

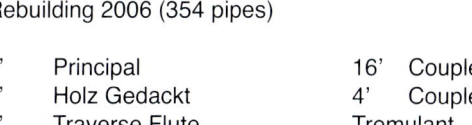

*Rebuilding 2006 (354 pipes)

8'	Principal	16'	Coupler
8'	Holz Gedackt	4'	Coupler
8'	Traverse Flute	Tremulant	
8'	Dulciana		
8'	Unda Maris TC	Crescendo pedal	
4'	Octave	No pedal organ	
4'	Traverse Flute	No presets	

St. Paul Evangelical Lutheran Church
146 Tamarack Street, Laurium, MI 49913
Phone: (906) 337-0231

Church History

The St. Paul congregation formed in 1879 and built the first church on Scott Street in Calumet. In 1887, an addition was added to serve as a school.

The present building on Tamarack Street was built and dedicated in 1899. Parochial school classes continued in the basement of the present church until 1905, when a new school was built on First Street in Laurium. The Great Depression caused many families to leave the area; enrollment dropped considerably, and the school was closed in 1929. During the first quarter century of the church, the German language was used exclusively. In 1917 the congregation became all English-speaking.

Organ History

Schuelke, 1902; rebuilt by Verlinden Co., 1963

The Schuelke tracker organ was given to the congregation in 1902 by Mr. Ernest Bollman. In 1929, two recitals were performed by Mr. Martin of Chicago to celebrate the 50th anniversary of the church. In 1961 Rudolf Patsloff donated

the trumpet rank, which is mounted to the left of the chancel in the front of the church.

Frank Ziems, organist for many years, left a bequest to renovate the organ. Renovation was completed by Verlinden Company of Milwaukee, in October 1963. The dedicatory recital was played by Rev. Harvey Gustafson of Minneapolis. He played four more recitals after that time. The chimes were given in memory of John Messner. The casework of the chamber is the work of Arthur Jarvela. (Source: Jan List)

Placement: rear balcony, right side of console faces the front of the sanctuary.

GREAT
8'	Diapason	4'	Great
8'	Melodia		Great Unison Off
8'	Dulciana	16'	Swell
4'	Principal	8'	Swell to Great
III	Mixture	4'	Swell to Great
8'	Trumpet		Chimes
16'	Great		Tremulant

SWELL
8'	Geigen	8'	Krummhorn
8'	Bourdon	8'	Trumpet
8'	Salicional	4'	Fagotto
8'	Celeste	16'	Swell
4'	Harmonic Flute	4'	Swell
2'	Fifteenth		Swell Unison Off
II	Sesquialtera Chimes		
16'	Krummhorn		Tremulant

PEDAL
16' Bourdon
8'   Octave Bass
4'   Fagotto
8'   Great to Pedal
4'   Great to Pedal
4'   Great to Pedal

Presets are inside the organ chamber.

Keweenaw Heritage Center at St. Anne's
(Former St. Anne's Catholic Church)
Corner of Scott & Fifth Streets, Calumet, MI 49913
Phone: (906) 337-2704

Church History

French Canadian Catholic immigrants built St. Anne's Church in 1900. The structure was built of red sandstone from the Jacobsville quarry, and many of the church's details are derived from the flamboyant or rayonnant style of the late Gothic period in France.

Deconsecrated in 1966, the church had been vacant or underutilized for more than three decades. In 1994, the Keweenaw Heritage Center at St. Anne's reversed this pattern of neglect that threatened one of Calumet's most significant and dominant structures. The Keweenaw Heritage Center highlights the social history of Michigan's Copper Country with exhibits, events and musical performances each summer.

Organ History

Barckhoff 2M, 16 ranks, 1899 Tracker. Hand pump preserved. Restored in 2009, Lauck Organ Co.

The Barckhoff Pipe Organ was built in 1899 for the Carmel Lutheran Church in Calumet. When the church was closed in the mid-1960s the organ was given to retired Pastor John Simonson. Pastor

Simonson rebuilt the organ in his home at Dollar Bay, Michigan. Upon his death, the family donated the organ to the Keweenaw Heritage Center at St. Anne's.

Restoration of the pipe organ began in 2007 and was finished in 2009 with the help of many volunteers—over 700 hours of volunteer labor and generous donors. Jim Lauck of the Lauck Organ Co. in Otsego, Michigan, directed the restoration effort. (Source: Anita Campbell)

GREAT
16'	Bourdon	49
8'	Open Diapason	61
8'	Viola Di Camba	61
8'	Doppel Flute	61
8'	Dulciana	61
4'	Principal	61
3'	Twelfth	61
2'	Fifteenth	

SWELL
8'	Violin Diapason	61
8'	Salicionale	61
8'	Stopped Diapason	61
4'	Fugara	61
4'	Flute Harmonic	61
2'	Piccolo	61

PEDAL
16'	Sub Base	27
8'	Flute Major	27

COMBINATION PEDALS
Great Organ Forte
Great Organ Piano
Balanced Swell Pedal

MECHANICAL REGISTERS
Great to Pedal
Swell to Pedal
Swell to Great
Bellows Signal, Tremolo, Wind Indicator

Operated by piston knobs placed below their respective manuals.

Community Church of Calumet
201 Red Jacket Road, Calumet, MI 49913
Phone: (906) 281-3494
(No longer a congregation—building now is The Calumet Art Center)

Church History

The Calumet Congregational Church was the church of Calumet and Hecla mining managers James MacNaughton and Alexander Agassiz and represented the elite and wealthy of the community. The original church, built in 1874, burned down in 1949. In 1971 the congregation merged with the Calumet Presbyterian Church, which had been built in 1894 to serve the Scottish Presbyterians in the area. The merged churches, first named the Federated Church, then became the Community Church of Calumet (Congregational-Presbyterian).

Calumet Art Center

In June of 2009, the Calumet Art Center, a nonprofit organization, bought the building that now houses the Art Center. The lower floor contains the studios for classes and the sanctuary is used as the performance area. The Art Center is open year-round to provide a safe learning environment where art, culture, and history inspire and challenge the people of the Keweenaw.

Organ History

Estey tracker 1907; rebuilt by Verlinden "incorporating most of the stops from the original organ," electro-pneumatic, 1970, 2M/28 stops, 16 ranks.

The organ was originally built from two Estey trackers from Brattleboro, Vermont. Estey was in business from 1846-1960 and manufactured more than

3,200 pipe organs during the first half of the 20th century. On November 5, 1969, the Verlinden Organ Company of Milwaukee removed the Calumet organ. Roman J. Leese, president of Verlinden, designed a new chamber and reinstalled the organ with most of the original pipes on July 13, 1970. It was converted to electro-pneumatic, and the console was moved from next to the chamber to a well at the opposite side of the choir loft. It is totally under expression. The first service with the new installation was played July 17, 1970, with James Abrams at the console. Dedicatory recitalist on November 5, 1970, was Harvey L. Gustafson. (Source: church records by Charles Stetter, Ed Gray)

GREAT (enclosed)
8'	Open Diapason	61 pipes
8'	Melodia	61 pipes
8'	Dulciana	61 pipes
4'	Octave	61 pipes
4'	Waldflote	12 pipes
2'	Fifteenth	12 pipes
II	Grave Mixture	122 pipes
8'	Trumpet	61 notes
16'	Great to Great	
4'	Great to Great	
8'	Swell to Great	
4'	Swell to Great	
	Four combination pistons	

SWELL (enclosed)
16'	Bourdon	73 notes
8'	Stopped Diapason	73 pipes
8'	Salicional	73 pipes
8'	Voix Celeste 'FC	49 pipes
4'	Principal	73 pipes
4'	Flute d'Amour	12 pipes
4'	Salicet	61 notes
22/3'	Nazard	61 notes
2'	Principal	61 notes
2'	Flautino	61 notes
13/5'	Tierce	57 notes
8'	Trumpet	73 pipes
4'	Clarion	61 notes
	Tremolo	
16'	Swell to Swell	
4'	Swell to Swell	
	Swell to Unison Off	
	Four combination pistons	

PEDAL (enclosed)
16'	Bourdon	32 pipes
16'	Lieblich Gedeckt	12 pipes
8'	Octave	12 pipes
8'	Base Flute	32 notes
8'	Gedeckt	32 notes
4'	Choral Bass	32 notes
8'	Trumpet	32 notes
8'	Great to Pedal	
8'	Swell to Pedal	
4'	Great to Pedal	

Deagan Chimes - 21 bells

Crescendo pedal
Sforzando toe piston
Great to pedal reversible toe piston
Expression pedal for entire organ

31

St. Paul the Apostle Catholic Church
301 Eighth Street, Calumet, MI 49913
Phone: (906) 337-2044

Church History

St. Joseph parish was established in 1889 by Slovenian immigrants. The original 1890 wood frame building was destroyed by fire in 1902. Construction of the new twin-spired, Jacobsville sandstone church designed by Charles Shand was begun in 1903. The interior, designed by Paul MacNeil, was completed in 1908. The building cost over $100,000.

By 1928, St. Joseph had absorbed the nearby St. Anthony of Padua Polish parish. In 1966, the four remaining ethnic parishes in Calumet were closed, including St. Joseph, and a new amalgamated parish was created in the former St. Joseph church building, named St. Paul the Apostle.

Organ History

Kilgen, 1905, reverse tracker, 2M, 17 stops. Hand pump preserved.

Dedicated on May 31, 1908, the organ cost $4,000. It was a gift to the church from a society of young men of the parish,

the Zveza Slovenskih Fantov, which was stenciled onto the pipes. The organ was built by Kilgen & Sons of St. Louis. It is 18' wide, 19' deep, 18' high at the sides and 12' high in the center. It has two manuals, a compass of CC to C, 61 notes each and a pedal compass of CCC to F of 30 notes each. It has 22 stops, 962 pipes and six pedal movements. The console is reversed. The original 1908 electric blower and back-up hand pump have been preserved, and are still in use. This tracker organ with pneumatic pedal was rebuilt and cleaned, its manuals were regulated, one stop was added, and new trackers were installed by Lauck in 2001. Pneumatic pedal, hand pump preserved. (Source: church brochure)

Placement: rear balcony, facing front of sanctuary

GREAT
8' Open Diapason
8' Trompette*
8' Melodia
4' Octave
4' Flute d'Amour
2' Fifteenth
16' Bourdon

SWELL (enclosed)
8' Violin Diapason
8' Salicional
8' Aeoline
8' Oboe Gamba (2 ranks, non-reed)
8' Stopped Diapason
4' Violina
4' Flute Harmonique
2' Flautina
    Swell to Great
    Tremolo

PEDAL
16' Bourdon
8' Violon Cello
    Great to Pedal
    Swell to Pedal
Pneumatic assist
Five foot pedals: soft to loud

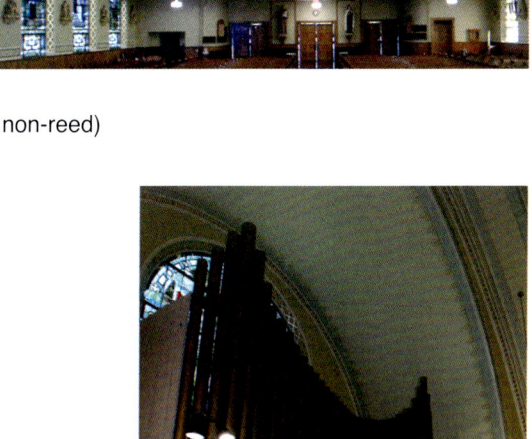

About the Authors

Anita Campbell has been fascinated with the historic pipe organs of the Keweenaw ever since she embarked on the restoration of the 1899 Barckhoff pipe organ at the Keweenaw Heritage Center at St. Anne's in Calumet, Michigan, in 2006.

Jan Dalquist did extensive research about the local pipe organs back in 2006 and published an in-depth article in the February 2007 issue of *The Diapason* magazine—a highly respected international monthly publication devoted to the organ, the harpsichord, carillon, and church music.

When Anita became aware of all the area pipe organs and Jan's 2007 *Diapason* article, it became her mission to publish Jan's article in more detailed booklet form. Both Jan and Anita felt it was important to promote these historic treasures in the community and acknowledge the preservation and maintenance effort that has been put into these instruments by local churches and organizations. It is hoped that visitors and musicians from outside the area will also enjoy learning about these historic pipe organs and the churches and organizations that house and preserve them.

View of mechanical workings of a tracker organ. Photo by Kevin Shawbitz.